AN ACCIDENT

Lydia Stryk

BROADWAY PLAY PUBLISHING INC
224 E 62nd St, NY NY 10065-8201
212 772-8334 fax: 212 772-8358
BroadwayPlayPubl.com

First printing December 2010
I S B N: 978-0-88145-476-5

Book design: Marie Donovan
Page make-up: Adobe Indesign
Typeface: Palatino
Printed and bound in the U S A

ABOUT THE AUTHOR

Lydia Stryk was born in DeKalb, Illinois and grew up between DeKalb and London, England, where she trained to be an actress at the Drama Centre. She went on to study history and journalism and then received a doctorate in theatre from the Graduate Center of the City University of New York. Her plays, including MONTE CARLO, THE HOUSE OF LILY, THE GLAMOUR HOUSE and AMERICAN TET (published by B P P I), have been part of festivals nationwide and in Europe and produced at theatdrs across the country including Denver Center Theater, Steppenwolf Theater Company, Victory Gardens, the Magic Theater and in Germany at Theaterhaus Stuttgart, Schauspiel Essen and the English Theatre Berlin. She is the recipient of a Berilla Kerr Playwriting Award and received the 2010 Rella Lossy Playwriting Award for AN ACCIDENT.

AN ACCIDENT premiered at the Magic Theater (Artistic Director, Loretta Greco) in San Francisco, California on 21 April 2010. The cast and creative contributors were:

LIBBY..Arwen Anderson
ANTON...Tim Kniffin

Director.. Rob Melrose
Sets & costumes..Erik Flatmo
Sound..Sara Huddleston
Lighting.. York Kennedy
Dramaturge..Jayne Benjulian

CHARACTERS & SETTING

Libby
Anton

Yes, a hospital room. And a bench outside.

AUTHOR'S NOTE

Well over a million people die in accidents every
year around the world, but many more survive with
various injuries of body, mind and spirit. Seven years
ago, I was hit and run over in a traffic accident on my
bike, joining others on the far side of one of life's great
divides. I discovered that accident survivors live in the
world in a different way. The life and death scenario
of the accident, itself, is of course dramatic in ways the
process of recovery is not. But there is something in the
latter that is compelling on its own terms—and never-
ending. And yet it was not until recently that I was able
to imagine writing this play. For it was then that the
idea of a relationship evolved to tell the story.

for Austin Pendleton

Scene

(A woman lies in a bed.)

LIBBY: "She's waking up. Her eyes flickered." Someone said that. I heard them. They said they saw my eyes *flicker*. Well, I *flinched*. That's what I did. I flinched.
(She turns her eyes toward the door.)
Because YOU *came too close*! I didn't *flicker*, okay? Let's just get that straight.
I flinched. Poke something in someone's eye. They flinch.
But you're right. I'm awake. You're perfectly right there.
(Looking around with her eyes)
I'm back. Back from. There.
Shadows. Softness. Echos. Someone asked me if I wanted to stay. I said no way. But I was trapped there, see? I was cramped there. I was trying to stretch and bend and find a room for myself. Find a way to stand up, lean forward, reach up. Get out. Hearing voices, noises. And then a door opened. And there was light.
(A pause)
If I could just lift my hands everything would be all right. Everything in the world would be all right.
(She studies her right hand.)
If I could just lift my right hand.
Maybe I can. I'll just give it a try.
(She wills herself mentally. Nothing moves.)
Well, maybe later.

I had a dream that a strange man was in my room.
Oh, God. Oh, fuck.

Something terrible's happened. Something very bad,
it seems, has happened to me. I wonder what it was. I
wonder what it was

I'm a little scared just now. A little scared.

Where's my foot? There it is. The other one is there.
Hands attached to arms. Toes attached to feet. Feet
to...? Where's my body? It's gone. There's a big hole in
the middle of me. Nothing's there.

This isn't nice. This isn't very fun. Someone has to help
me. Someone has to come.

God.

Well, well. So. Ain't life a bitch. Well, well. So, so, so.

You've got your mind. You know who you are. The
name escapes me right now, but that's not a problem.
I know who I am. And I am in a hospital room. This
is a hospital room. That's clear. No doubt about that.
There's no one here right now. But somebody will
come.

There was a man here. But he's gone now. He was
sitting over in that corner.

So. I don't have a body, folks. I don't have a body. The
body's lying on the bed, here, under my head. But I
don't *have* it, you understand? I, uh. I don't have it.
I don't seem to. I can't. Move. I can't move it. I can't
move.

I can't move. I can't move.

It'll be fine. I'll be fine. It'll be okay. It'll be fine. No
need to panic. Life throws some funny curves, doesn't
it?

If I could just move my toe. Wait! It moved. It moved.
I moved my toe! I'm saved, I'm saved. I am. I am. I can
wiggle my big toe. I can.

(Pause)

On my *right* foot...
That's something. I'm going to hold on to that. That's
hopeful.
*(She looks around with her eyes, taking in her surroundings.
Her head and neck remian immobile. She spots the window.)*
I've got a view. Things are looking up! There's a canal
out there. And benches along it, look at that. There's a
sculpture. A bird of some kind. A big metal bird with
metal wings. Or maybe it's a plane! No, it's Superman!
And people. Would you look at that. Walking. Look
at that. One leg, then the other, walking. That one's
running. Gallump, gallump. That one's swaggering.
(Imitating him) "Big man, look at me." Lovers. Bumping
into each other as they walk, like drunkards. Drunk
on love. There's a man sitting on a bench. He's got
his hands in his pockets. Sitting there. Probably gone
crazy. Worn down by life. You'd have to be crazy to
sit still. With your hands in your pockets. When you
could be moving. Take your hands out of your pocket,
man! Get up!
If I could sit up.
(Pause)
If I could just. Sit up. I would give everything.
Everything in the world. Maybe I can.
(A pause, she tries.)
Well, maybe another day.
Don't panic.
Libby.
(A smile alights her face.)
That's my name.
(End of scene)

Scene

(A man sits on a bench with his hands in his pockets.)

ANTON: Stopped off at the store. When it's this hot a supermarket feels like a good bet. I didn't need anything. *I bought cherries!* Giant things. Popped one in my mouth. Crunch, crunch. Pulled out. I was thinking about. How good they tasted. Crisp and sweet. But that it wasn't how a cherry was supposed to taste. In fact, they tasted like something else entirely. Like cherry candy. I was picturing a garden from when I was a kid, and how cherries—

And I heard a scream. And then a thump. And then everything went silent. And there was this woman lying there. And she wasn't moving. This can't be happening went through my head. People fall, they get up. They cuss you out. They dust themselves off. They stumble away. This woman lay there with her eyes closed. And her head was bleeding, red as cherries on to the shimmering asphalt of the parking lot. And most of her was under my car.

This woman's body had found its way under my Toyota Corolla. What I am about to say. You can believe this. I'm just terrible at lying. So you can believe this. I lifted the car off of her. I lifted it up and pushed her away. I kicked her away like a doll. A rag doll. Out from under my car. Look at me. And you don't believe in miracles?

And then I went into shock.

The woman under the car was very badly injured. A fluke accident, they call it. Pulling out of a supermarket parking lot, I hit her, and she lost her balance and fell and hit her head and it was then that I crushed her with the wheels of my car. Unconscious from the fall, she felt nothing.

I didn't need those cherries. Don Chevise was in there, standing over the freezer. Studying the ice cream. Why didn't I stop to say hello? If I'd gone straight home. If it hadn't been so damned hot.

I teach history sixth period, and I rush home. After 6th period, you need to recover. I put my feet up with a good book. I read histories of wars and generals' biographies. That's where I should have been.

(End of scene)

Scene

(A man is sitting in the corner of the room.)

LIBBY: You're the man who's been sitting in the corner of my room.

Who let you in?

ANTON: I'm sorry. I didn't want to disturb you. I'll just go.

LIBBY: No. I want to know. Who let you in?

ANTON: No one stopped me.

(He stands.)

LIBBY: Who are you?

ANTON: I'm the one who.

LIBBY: You're the one who...?

ANTON: Hit you.

LIBBY: Oh, oh! They told me about you.

(She looks away from him.)

That's unkind. That's not nice. You're the jerk who ruined my life? You're him?

ANTON: That's me. I just needed

LIBBY: You needed. I'm the one with needs here, mister. Let's get that straight.

ANTON: Yes, yes.

LIBBY: Well, go on.

ANTON: I wanted you to know—

LIBBY: —Know what? How sorry you is? Is that it? That you didn't mean it?

ANTON: To *know*. Who did this to you. I did this to you. I did this. To you. I'm the one. It was me. I'm the one who did this terrible, unforgivable thing. To you. I just wanted you to know.

(A long pause. She looks at him.)

LIBBY: Oh. Okay. That's okay then.

(ANTON continues to stand. LIBBY observes him.)

ANTON: In case, well, I think I would want to know. I would have wanted to know. And to hear from that person that they understood. Understood what they had done.
You're back. You've come back now. I was waiting for this moment.

(LIBBY says nothing. She continues to observe ANTON. He sinks on to his knees and bows his head in a spontaneous act of penance.)

LIBBY: Get up.

(ANTON stands, waits.)

LIBBY: Turn around.

(ANTON does so, making a slow circle.)

LIBBY: Come nearer.

(ANTON advances, slowly.)

LIBBY: Stop.

(ANTON stops.)

LIBBY: Lift your left hand.

(ANTON *does.*)

LIBBY: Lift your right hand.

(ANTON *does.*)

LIBBY: Lift your right foot.

Left foot.

Right foot.

Left.

Right.

Left.

Right! Left! Right, Left! Right/left/right/left/right/left/right/left

(ANTON *marches in place, his hands up as if under arrest and his feet marching in rhythm with her commands. This goes on for some time.*)

LIBBY: Stop!

(ANTON *stops. A pause.*)

LIBBY: You can leave now.

(ANTON *does not move.*)

(*End of scene*)

Scene

(ANTON, *on the bench*)

ANTON: There was blunt trauma to the spinal column. Resulting in damage to the vertebrae. At this stage they can't rule out the suspicion of spinal chord injury. She's still in shock. Her body's not moving. The swelling is putting pressure on her nervous system, so no one can say if it's permanent or temporary. And her pelvis is shattered. And her left foot is smashed. And she has massive bruising. And three broken ribs. She has chances for recovery. But no one can say for sure how

much she will recover. They just don't know. If she
will walk again. They don't know yet, if she will sit up
again. She's in surgery now. They've collapsed a lung.
Cutting through the chest cavity to reach the vertebrae.
(A pause, there's more.)
And there was brain trauma. So she can't remember
what it was that happened to her. Months—maybe
years— of her life have disappeared. The doctors count
on significant recovery there. But they won't say how
much or how long it will take.
She lets me visit her.
She jokes around.
Tells the nurses we met 'by accident'. "But then, there
are no accidents, are there?" she says. She's remarkably
cheerful. It's the morphine in large part, I know.
(A pause)
It's not all fun and games, though.
She seems to have no one in the city. She can't
remember how she got here. At some point in life,
you've got to take responsibility. Since the accident,
I've had very little time. She'll see me for a little while.
She can't take much more in the way of company. It
exhausts her. And then I come out here and sit. I can
see up into her room. And when the lights go out, I go
home.
I say a prayer for her to the air, the moon.
And I am preparing for her rage. Without armor.
(End of scene)

Scene

(ANTON sits by LIBBY's bedside. They sit wordless for some time.)

LIBBY: Are you married, Anton? Gay?

ANTON: Divorced.

LIBBY: Oh. I see.
I don't know what I am.

ANTON: *(Affirming, awkward)* No.

LIBBY: You see, my memory's a little shaky.

(ANTON nods.)

LIBBY: I seem to forget.

ANTON: *(Trying, helpless)* You're not alone in that.

LIBBY: I'm not?

ANTON: *(Getting himself in deeper)* But I have no excuse. For my forgetfulness.

LIBBY: Forget to watch the road sometimes?

(ANTON bows his head.)

LIBBY: So what do you do?

ANTON: I teach history.

LIBBY: I see.

ANTON: The civil war is my, uh, main field of study.

LIBBY: Oh, yeah?
(Looking him over)
Any children?

ANTON: One daughter. She's in med school now.

LIBBY: You must be very proud of her.
(Pause)
Did you tell her about me?

ANTON: She knows about you.

LIBBY: What did you tell her about the accident?

ANTON: I told her—

LIBBY: What happened.

ANTON: Right.

LIBBY: What happened, Anton?

ANTON: You really?

LIBBY: Tell me. I want to hear it in your words.

(A pause)

ANTON: I bought a few groceries.

LIBBY: What kind?

ANTON: Oh, nothing much. The whole thing. It wasn't necessary.

LIBBY: You don't remember what you bought?

ANTON: Yes, I do. As a matter of fact. I bought cherries.

LIBBY: Cherries. Were they good? Were they sweet?

ANTON: They were sweet and good.

LIBBY: A good cherry is hard to find these days. And then?

ANTON: I pulled out of the lot.

(A pause)

LIBBY: You had to have those cherries, didn't you, Anton?

ANTON: No.

LIBBY: Thank you. Now I know.
(She nods.)
Now I know what happened.
Did you tell her the rest of it? Your daughter? That we're "seeing each other"?

ANTON: No, I did not.

LIBBY: And why not? You're not close or something?

ANTON: Yes, we are.

LIBBY: Then, why?

ANTON: I can't explain it.

LIBBY: To her? You can't explain it to her or to yourself?

ANTON: To either.

LIBBY: But you share my medical details, don't you?

ANTON: Yes.

LIBBY: I'm something of a text-book case for her, aren't I? Full of glorious, gory detail. Reason enough to keep you coming here. A sort of bonding with her.

ANTON: You're angry.

LIBBY: I don't know why I put up with you. How much longer will my case be interesting?

ANTON: I've hurt you.

LIBBY: No. Come on, I love being a cripple!

ANTON: I meant to tell her.

LIBBY: What's her name? She hasn't got a name.

ANTON: She's got a name.

LIBBY: So, what is it?

ANTON: It's Laura.

LIBBY: Laura. That's a pretty name. And your wife?

ANTON: Ex-wife. Judy.
I just haven't found the words—

LIBBY: The catheter's back in again.

ANTON: I never meant to—

LIBBY: I've got some kind of infection.

(ANTON's stopped.)

LIBBY: I'm tired. I'm losing my will.

(*A long pause*)

I don't understand why you keep coming here.

(ANTON *says nothing.*)

LIBBY: I release you.

I beg you to go and never come back. Your presence is unhealthy for me. The doctors told me to tell you. You bring the accident up in me. Over and over. I can't stand the sight of you. Your sad face. You bore me. You exhaust me. I need to heal and you won't let me. You like me like this. You love that I suffer. You get off on it, in some kinky way—

(ANTON *grabs* LIBBY's *arm, she screams with pain. He collapses.*)

ANTON: Oh, god.

LIBBY: (*Suddenly*) Wait.

ANTON: Libby?

LIBBY: Do that again. What you just did.

(ANTON *gets up and very tentatively, gently, takes hold of* LIBBY's *arms.*)

LIBBY: Harder.

(ANTON *does as she asks.* LIBBY *is very quiet.*)

LIBBY: Tighter.

(ANTON *does so. It is clear that he is using full strength. In a burst he intensifies his hold and then releases. But he continues to hold on to* LIBBY. *She is very still.*)

LIBBY: Anton.

ANTON: Yes?

LIBBY: I can feel my body again.

(ANTON *continues to hold* LIBBY.)

(*End of scene*)

Scene

(LIBBY *is looking out the window.* ANTON *sits by her bedside.*)

LIBBY: Did you know trees talk to each other, Anton?

ANTON: No, Libby, I didn't, no.

LIBBY: They do. They speak in waves. They send out cries of alarm and comfort. They also tell the future. If you listen closely to them. That's what I read. They are wiser than we are and they see ahead. I never wanted to know the future, did you?

ANTON: I take that stuff for a lot of hocus pocus.

LIBBY: Not me. That's why I avoid it. Fortune tellers and their ilk. That's the last thing I would ever have wanted. The last thing I'd have needed. To know this was coming? Would you have liked to know this was coming, Anton?

ANTON: (*Softly*) No. Not if it was unavoidable. I am glad I didn't know. What am I saying, I don't believe in any of that. Libby.

LIBBY: But if I had. I would have done it differently. I would have lived another life, for sure.

ANTON: Don't think like that, Libby.

LIBBY: Why not?

ANTON: It doesn't bear thinking about. I've thought it through—

LIBBY: You're not the thought police. You're not the only one who thinks.
(*A pause*)
(*Thinking*) But if you knew what was in store. Then what would be the point in living?

ANTON: No...point.

But. Well, we all know what's coming.

LIBBY: I like mystery.

ANTON: *(Helpless)* Yes. No. Maybe...

LIBBY: Have you heard of the wild apple forest of Kazakhstan? Anton? I read about it in a magazine. Genetic evidence suggests that the world's first apples grew there. The apple was born in that forest! That must make it the true Garden of Eden. I want to see that forest. If it's the last thing I do.

ANTON: You will then.

LIBBY: I want to bite into a wild apple. And then I'll know, won't I? I'll have the knowledge necessary to continue. Do you believe in fate, Anton?

ANTON: I'm too rational for that. I don't *believe* in anything. Except, well, cause, effect. And the occasional miracle.

LIBBY: They say things happen for a reason. I don't think so. I see no evidence for that. I see no reason for *this*.

ANTON: We invent reasons, Libby. After the fact.

LIBBY: I should have climbed Mount Kilimanjaro. I really wanted to do that, you know? I should have tried to save the world. While I had the chance. I wanted to storm a primate research center, Anton. That's really what I should have been doing. When this thing happened. I was a news junkie, Anton. I know it's hard to believe. A head line addict. I was a concerned citizen of the world.

ANTON: I believe it, why wouldn't I? I believe it one hundred percent. Why are you speaking in the past tense?

LIBBY: Do I look like a news junkie?

ANTON: I can read you the papers! I'll go and get—

LIBBY: Sit down, Anton. You're like a jack-in-the-box. Always jumping up and down.

(ANTON *sits.*)

LIBBY: I see news flashes. In my head. News flashes, Anton. From the past. That's all that's left. I had the news on, the internet on. I had to know right then. I had to follow it all. I was plugged in. Connected. I feel sure that I was twittering. And I was angry. Who wouldn't be? But I don't need to hear it now. It all comes down to the same thing. Broken bodies. It starts and ends with the body, that's all.
Now I know.
A body is a miracle, Anton. It's sacred. Can't we start from there?
I loved to run in the morning and dance at night. Or to dance in the morning and run at night. Sometimes I'd run and dance at the same time. Do you like to dance?

ANTON: I have two left feet.

LIBBY: Everyone can dance.

ANTON: With the rare exceptions.

LIBBY: Turn on the radio, Anton. Find me a good station.

(ANTON *fumbles with the radio.*)

ANTON: What kind of music, do you—

LIBBY: (*Impatient*) Just do it! I'll say when to stop—

(ANTON *obeys* LIBBY. *As the dial hits a hard-core techno dance beat—something like Dr Baker's Kaos...*)

LIBBY: Stop!

(ANTON *stops.*)

LIBBY: Louder!

(ANTON *makes it louder.* LIBBY *listens. Her eyes seem to glisten. Her face seems to dance.)*

LIBBY: Get up and dance, Anton!

ANTON: No.

Don't. Libby. No. I can't.

LIBBY: Dance, go on. Dance, Anton. Damn it!

ANTON: *(Getting up)* I don't know how—-

LIBBY: Just move your body!

ANTON: *(Standing, helplessly)* I can't move

LIBBY: How dare you say that to me? You can't move! You fucker! How dare you say that to me! *(She begins to hyperventilate.)* Dance, you fucker!

(With a gesture of despair ANTON *begins to dance. He can't dance, but the music enters his body. It enters his hands, arms, torso, feet. He dances. He lets himself be carried away. It is beautiful. This goes on for some time.* LIBBY *watches him.)*

(End of scene)

Scene

(LIBBY *and* ANTON)

LIBBY: Being incapacitated has its advantages. I've been thinking them through. I just need to focus on them, luxuriate. It's like a vacation on the beach. It's like a long bath. Do you take baths, Anton?

ANTON: I couldn't start the day without one. A day has to start slowly. Under water. Floating.

LIBBY: I hate baths, in reality. The idea comes into your head— great, a long hot bath. That's what I need. That's just what the doctor ordered. With bubbles and oils. And you're all excited. And then you get into it and it's hot and you can't breathe and your body begins to shrivel and there are so many things you need to be doing and you feel like you're drowning. Drowning in your mother's womb or something.

ANTON: You're pulling through.

LIBBY: "Lucky to be alive", that's what they say. About people like me. No matter how bad it is. If you get out of it alive. If you're still breathing. Then you're lucky.

ANTON: You survived this. Do you know why?

LIBBY: I'm in agony.

ANTON: *(Keeping going)* You're a survivor. That's why.

LIBBY: The feelings came back. What I feel is pain.

ANTON: Without people like you there'd be no life on earth. There'd be no history

LIBBY: Like stabs. Like something's grinding me.

ANTON: *(Determined)*. History is made by survivors. Like you.

(A pause. LIBBY takes this in, she looks at ANTON.)

ANTON: Some survive the battle, Libby. Is all I'm saying.

LIBBY: I'm not a fucking soldier, Anton, from your history books. I didn't sign up for this.

ANTON: No. You didn't. But nevertheless. You made it.

LIBBY: War is not an accident.

ANTON: No. You're right, it's not.

LIBBY: This here's no battlefield. This ain't no victory.

ANTON: No, Libby.

LIBBY: And those who don't survive? What about them? That miracle window washer who fell forty-seven stories? He was walking his dog six months

later! But look at his poor brother. The unlucky
window-washer. No miracle for him. And it was the
wind that saved the one, not some fucking miracle. Or
it's the wind that's the miracle. A bowel movement is a
miracle. From where I'm laying. And his survival does
not make him a hero, okay? But his life might, but who
cares about that? Illegal immigrant. Well, he certainly
gave back-breaking work a new meaning!
All I'm saying is. I was lucky. I admit it. But it doesn't
make me special.
And it didn't have to be like that. Don't take comfort in
that.
I could be dead. Or a vegetable, is that what they call
it? And why do they call it that?
A vegetable. It's demeaning. Who dared to come up
with that.
(She lets out a sigh.)
I should have just died and done with it.

ANTON: Libby!

LIBBY: I'm not grateful, Anton. To have survived. I am
not grateful, you hear me? To be alive. I don't feel like
starting over with a new lease on life.
Besides, everyone loves an untimely death. You ever
notice that? And there's nothing we love better than
a tragic accident. That cosmic fate. That mother of all
bad luck. We can't get enough of it. Preferably, you're
taken in your prime, the more beautiful the better. A
princess, a sports hero, an actress. It's so riveting. So
damn unfathomable. It's so cathartic. So ancient Greek.
So primal. But survival? The damaged goods? We're
embarrassed by it. Tongue-tied. I know you're tongue-
tied, Anton. I see you struggling.

(ANTON turns away, hurt.)

LIBBY: Cheer up.

I'd trade places with you any day. If it makes you feel
any better.
I'd rather have hit *you*. Than be like this.
I'd rather have killed you.
Than this.

(ANTON *looks at* LIBBY.)

LIBBY: I hope that's a comfort.

ANTON: *(Slowly)* There was a witness. She was coming
towards you. She saw the whole thing.

(LIBBY *struggles to raise her head. She can. She listens
intently.*)

ANTON: You were running she says. Across the
highway. And at the same time, you were on your cell
phone, she says. Looking down, and texting.
Instead of looking where you were going.
If you'd have been looking, you'd have seen me
coming.
You'd have seen me coming in time to stop.
I take some comfort in that.

(End of scene)

Scene

(LIBBY, *alone*)

LIBBY: Here we are in the middle of the night. The night
is not your friend when you can't turn, can't lift.
Try to relax, Libby. What have you got to lose? Call
the night nurse for a pill. Why bother her? She's dozed
off at the desk. Well, she has the hardest job of all. The
terror on the ward at night is palpable. It has to get to
you. And the pills don't help anyway. They just give
you hallucinations.

Memories are like wicked children. They creep up
from behind you, they play hide and seek inside you.
Especially at night.

Calm down, Libby. For weeks now, you've been
waiting for the dawn. And doesn't she always come?
She always comes. And now you know what gratitude
is. Gratitude like I've never known before. Like I never
knew existed.

That's what it must have been like. For the first woman
and the first man. On the first morning. After the first
night on earth. I finally understand the Old Testament!
Waiting for the dawn and the dawn coming.

Focus on the dawn. She's an approaching, lover, Libby.
Let go, she'll be here soon.

It's the light. You feel it enter the sky. You feel it in
your chest, in your heart. Before you can see it, before
any visible sign.

*(She looks around the room, as if for something to occupy
her. She begins to sing Cole Porter's Night and Day. She
doesn't know most the words. After a time, she stops. The
song lingers in the air. A pause.)*

You'd think with all this time on my hands, I could
get a lot done. Plan a revolution. Devise a peace plan
for the Middle East. Count my blessings. Weigh my
options.

Calculate costs for my accident case. Compose a
sharp attack against the insurance company who will
inevitably refuse to pay me.

Write a novel in my head.

Or a memoir. Why not. They're really popular.

(She tries to remember. She gives up.)

Well, maybe another day.

(covering, defensively) I'm too busy, anyway. Too busy
waiting. Waiting for the morning.

Sometimes the nurse flips the light switch before dawn.
Yellow florescent light fills the room like a scream. It's
like acid thrown in your face.

But they don't mean to be cruel. I cried out once—used
a hefty expletive—and that nurse, boy, she wouldn't
talk to me for days.

That's not a place I would recommend being. On the
wrong side of a nurse. Believe you me.

I need to toss and turn. It's agony. Toss and turn. God,
help me.

*(She begins to toss her head from side to side, thrashing it.
She lets out a howl of agony. Then she grows still, waiting.)*

(Suddenly) Oh, oh. Here it comes.

(Dawn enters the room. This takes a very long time.)

Thank you, dawn. Thank you, day. I want to write you
a poem, wash your feet.

(As the room brightens, she closes her eyes and falls asleep.)

(End of scene)

Scene

(ANTON, *on the bench*)

ANTON: "You didn't hear a thing I said, did you?"
Judy'd say. And the truth is, I hadn't. My mind was
elsewhere. Throughout our marriage.

There are some damn large questions out there. You
start asking them and you're no longer really here.

"You're not here, Anton," she'd say. "I may as well be
on my own. Did you hear what I just said?"

"Judy?"

"I'm leaving, Anton."

To heal someone you have to be present.

I can heal her. I will heal her.

I've turned to the Shamans. I am reading about the luminous field of energy surrounding the body. Everything is there. Our fears, pain, all the damage. But the radiating humanity is there. The force of being which is energy and light.
And I've been reading how all the hurtful things can be extracted from it. Lifted out of the luminous field. According to ancient Inca tradition, we are all healers. We can heal if we are open. Becoming channels. Through our lifting hands.
I realize there is no scientific evidence for this practice, but I have decided to believe.
And I've begun a quest to be present in my life. I am hauling myself back. A practice that consumes my days now. Hauling myself back from the other world in my mind.

(End of scene)

Scene

(LIBBY *and* ANTON)

LIBBY: You didn't hear a thing I said, did you, Anton?

ANTON: Libby?

LIBBY: Why're you looking at me like that, Anton? Staring?

ANTON: Was I? Am I? Like what?

LIBBY: Like a devouring beast.

(ANTON *says nothing.*)

LIBBY: You want to make love to me, is that it?

ANTON: Libby!

LIBBY: Is that what you're trying to say?

ANTON: I was looking at your luminous field.

LIBBY: *Anton?*

ANTON: The energy field. Surrounding you. I'd like to. With my hands. I'd like to. Try to. Heal you. Can I try?

LIBBY: You were staring at my breasts.

ANTON: Libby! Please! I wasn't. I swear to you.

LIBBY: Oh, come on, Anton. I'm having fun. I'm teasing you.

ANTON: I don't think that's very funny.

LIBBY: I'd lift up my gown to show you, if I could. I'll let you look. For a price.

ANTON: What price, Libby?

LIBBY: Get me some rat poison. And you'll give it to me. If I ask you for it. You'll give it to me. And as much as I ask you for.

ANTON: Let me try?

LIBBY: Who was I texting? When you ran me over?

(ANTON *shrugs, helpless.*)

LIBBY: You ran over the damn phone, didn't you?

(ANTON *nods, yes.*)

LIBBY: Phone crushed. Memory crushed.

(*A long pause*)

Okay.

You can heal me now.

(ANTON *approaches* LIBBY. *Begins to roll up his sleeves*)

LIBBY: God, Anton. What are you doing? What's next? Are you getting out the knife?

ANTON: (*Quieting her*) Please?

(ANTON *holds out his hands, above* LIBBY's *body. He begins to feel her energy field through his hands. His hands bounce up and down, like a plane in turbulence, then still.*)

LIBBY: Your hands are beautiful. Anyone ever tell you that?

(ANTON *withdraws his hands.*)

LIBBY: No. Don't stop.

(ANTON *returns them.*)

LIBBY: You've got to learn to take a compliment.

(ANTON *is beginning again.*)

LIBBY: Don't tickle me, whatever else you do. I'm very ticklish.

(ANTON *rolls his eyes, they laugh, settle. He begins again.*)

LIBBY: Take off the gown.
(A pause)
(Matter-of-factly) If you don't, it won't work.

(LIBBY *closes her eyes as if the matter is settled and waits. At first* ANTON *seems unable to comply. But then he does, gently removing her gown. She is naked. He continues where he left off, with intense concentration, channeling healing energy. But very soon, he can't, he turns away. She opens her eyes.*)

LIBBY: Why'd you stop, Anton?

ANTON: I can't.

LIBBY: You can. I want you to.

ANTON: It's too much. Too beautiful.

LIBBY: It's just a body, Anton.

ANTON: A body is so beautiful.

LIBBY: A broken one.
I want you to kiss my body. I want you to kiss my breasts.

ANTON: I don't think you realize.

LIBBY: I'd like that very much.

ANTON: What you're asking of me. What you're doing, Libby, it's not a game.

LIBBY: Who said it was?

(ANTON *turns to* LIBBY *as if to protest, but he can't stop himself. He bends down, and with gentle control and bodily distance, kisses her body and then each breast. But then he is over her, burying his face in her breasts, intensely, then roughly. He stops abruptly and leaves. She turns her face to the window and looks out. After some time and with great focus, she lifts the fingers on her right hand one by one and the hand and then the arm. She studies it in the air.*)

(*End of scene*)

Scene

(*Time has passed.* ANTON *stands.* LIBBY *lies in bed.*)

LIBBY: You're back.

ANTON: I needed.

LIBBY: Days have gone by, I think.

ANTON: To think.

LIBBY: And nights.

ANTON: (*Attempting finality*)
I came today to say goodbye.

LIBBY: You run me over! You stalk me! You molest me! And now you want to leave me!

ANTON: Good bye, Libby.
(*He is leaving.*)

LIBBY: Look! Anton!
(*She sits up slowly, with great concentration, stretching her arms a little out towards him.*)
It worked. Your healing.

(ANTON *is stopped by this.*)

ANTON: Libby!

(*Taking a step toward her*)

Oh.

LIBBY: You did this.

ANTON: No. I only. *You.* You let yourself. Heal. Libby

(*A long pause.* ANTON *takes in* LIBBY's *upright body with astonishment. They both look at her lifted hands with some wonderment and then at each other. She lets her right arm drop. She reaches out her left hand.*)

LIBBY: Give me five, man.

(*Before* ANTON *can,* LIBBY *lets her left hand drop. She lies back down heavily.*)

ANTON: I almost didn't come back.

LIBBY: Just stay.

ANTON: I shouldn't have.

LIBBY: You had to.

ANTON: After that.

LIBBY: You had to come back, Anton.

ANTON: Had to? No.

LIBBY: You did, though.

(*That seems argument enough.* ANTON *sits. They stay together in silence. They are cautious with each other.*)

LIBBY: (*With a cheery normalcy*) So, how've you been? I mean apart from.

ANTON: Laura came home for a visit.

LIBBY: Oh, that must have been nice. Did you do something special?

ANTON: (*Insistent*) How are *you*? I mean, apart from. (*Gesturing to her body with wonder*)

LIBBY: *(Ignoring this)* Did you do something fun?

ANTON: *(Giving in)* We went for a walk.

LIBBY: That sounds like fun.

ANTON: We went out for dinner. She wanted to cook, but—

LIBBY: What'd you have?

(ANTON is stuck.)

LIBBY: You don't remember?

(ANTON searches, gives up, shakes his head.)

LIBBY: *(Shaking her head)* Anton, Anton.
How's school?

ANTON: She's preparing for exams. Exhausted but happy.

LIBBY: That must feel good. Anton?

ANTON: *(Surprised)* It does.

LIBBY: Raising a happy child is an accomplishment.
I had a happy childhood.

ANTON: You did, Libby? You remember it?

LIBBY: I remember. And I was happy, okay?

ANTON: Sure, Libby. I didn't mean—

LIBBY: It's how I got here I keep stumbling on.
(A pause)
Guess what? The police were here.

ANTON: The police?

LIBBY: They say I'm a "missing person". Well, they got that right.

ANTON: It's only a matter of time.

LIBBY: 'Til what?

ANTON: Until they find you.

LIBBY: Who?

ANTON: The people who love you.

(LIBBY *takes this in.*)

LIBBY: They asked me a lot of questions.

ANTON: Like what?

LIBBY: As if I was hiding. As if I was hiding something.
They were investigating. They searched my closet.
I may be missing, Anton.
(She is upset, worked up.)
But I know who I am.

(A pause, ANTON *bows his head.)*

LIBBY: *(Quickly)* I had a very happy childhood. It's not
something you want to admit to. It's embarrassing.
But I expect it's got me through. I was so free, Anton.
And fearless. The world was my oyster. At home, I was
spoiled with love.
And you?

ANTON: I think you can guess where I spent my
childhood.

LIBBY: In the local library.

ANTON: Bingo. I was asthmatic. And worried over
constantly. I found my adventure and freedom in the
library.
And I've never left it. Metaphorically.

LIBBY: Until now.

ANTON: *(He smiles.)* That's right.

LIBBY: *(Calming, now, settling in)* Tell me a story.

ANTON: What kind?

LIBBY: Something brutal, compelling, with a shocking
twist and a happy ending.
I don't care, Anton. Just make something up.

ANTON: Okay...
Once upon a t—-
LIBBY: —Whatever else you do, please don't start like
that.

ANTON: Well, why not?

LIBBY: Let it be about the future.

ANTON: A science fiction kind of thing?

LIBBY: No. A fairy tale set in the future.

ANTON: Oh, jeez.
So how does a fairy tale set in the future start?

LIBBY: One day ...

ANTON: One day

LIBBY: A hundred years from now and very far away

ANTON: A child will be born

LIBBY: No, Anton.

ANTON: No?

LIBBY: Not a child. Every one expects a child to born.
Something else. Let something else be born.

ANTON: Like what, Libby?

LIBBY: It's your story.

(End of scene)

Scene

*(LIBBY is lying flat on her back, covered by a sheet up to her
neck. ANTON is half-in, half-out of the room.)*

LIBBY: Come in, Anton. Don't hover by the door.

ANTON: But—

LIBBY: You're like a humming bird. Hovering there.
Waiting for nectar.

ANTON: But. You're not up yet, Libby. I can come back—

LIBBY: *Au contraire.* I am *up*! And feeling wonderful today. Never felt better, in fact. Come in. Sit down.

(ANTON *does so, cautiously.*)

LIBBY: I woke up this morning thinking positive thoughts! I am a survivor! On the road to recovery. There's more than light at the end of this girl's tunnel— there's victory!

ANTON: Libby!

LIBBY: April Fool's, Anton!

(LIBBY *smiles widely at* ANTON. *He sinks perceptibly. A pause.*)

LIBBY: My body's not moving.

ANTON: What? Libby?

LIBBY: It'll be okay. It'll be fine. I guess I overdid things, Anton.

ANTON: (*Jumping up, reacting to the news*) God. No.

LIBBY: Just need to take it a bit more slowly. Take my time.

ANTON: How. Oh—

LIBBY: It's only temporary. A temporary relapse. That's what they're saying.

ANTON: What can I—

LIBBY: (*Suddenly*) I brought you a present!

ANTON: A present? Libby? What—

LIBBY: On the table, Anton. One of the nurses brought it in for me.

(ANTON *looks at* LIBBY *lying there, searching her for answers, and then at the table top, covered in objects.*)

LIBBY: My table. My whole world. The paper bag, Anton.

(ANTON *takes the paper bag, hesitates.*)

LIBBY: Well, open it.

(ANTON *opens the bag.*)

ANTON: Cherries.

LIBBY: They're from this nurse's garden. She picked them for me.

(ANTON *studies them. He looks at* LIBBY.)

LIBBY: Try one.
They're washed. I had the nurse wash them.

(ANTON *offers the bag to* LIBBY.)

LIBBY: No. They're for you.

(*A pause.* ANTON *sits. Another pause and then he begins to eat the cherries.* LIBBY *watches him.*)

LIBBY: Good?

(ANTON *nods. He eats the cherries slowly,* LIBBY *watches. This goes on for some time. After the fourth or fifth cherry, it's clear that the cherries are affecting him. He stops, rushes out of the room, the bag falling onto the floor. We hear him heaving, sick to his stomach. After a time, he comes back in, stands at the door. He appears shaken.*)

LIBBY: What happened? What's wrong, Anton?

ANTON: Nothing.

LIBBY: Nothing? You don't look good.

(ANTON *wipes his mouth with his sleeve. He catches a breath.*)

ANTON: Everything's fine. I'm fine, Libby.
(*He summons a jolly, terrifying smile.*)

LIBBY: Well, that's okay, then. We're both fine.

(She begins to laugh and cannot stop.)

(End of scene)

Scene

(LIBBY sits propped up on her bed. ANTON is on his feet. He is teaching.)

ANTON: The battle begins at dawn. And by five-thirty in the afternoon, it's all over. And twenty-three thousand men are lying dead or injured on the "bloody cornfield," as they called it. Sharpsburg was the single bloodiest day in American military history.

LIBBY: You must be a good teacher, Anton.

ANTON: *(Not sure what to make of this)* Thanks. Shall I go on?

(LIBBY nods, yes.)

ANTON: In Gettysburg, it was the same thing. Confederate General George E. Pickett sent thirteen thousand troops across an open field to penetrate Union lines. Ten thousand men killed or wounded in under an hour. Pickett's charge was the bloodiest *hour* of the war.

LIBBY: Gosh.

ANTON: *(Patiently)* Shall I continue?

LIBBY: Yeah. Go on.

ANTON: And after every battle, the armies, what was left of them, would move on. But the injured were left to heal eventually or die. The suffering was unimaginable. Antibiotics weren't invented yet. Water was scarce. Infection and disease were rampant. Soldiers with body wounds were just left to die. There was nothing to be done for them. But for those with wounds to the arms and legs, well, there was amputation. The surgeons had little choice. And they became good at it. They could complete an amputation in under ten minutes.—

(LIBBY *raises her hand.*)

ANTON: *(Calling on her)* Yes, Libby?

LIBBY: But you would die from the pain.

ANTON: Well, they had chloroform. But it was often unavailable. So, you're right. The pain would have been unbearable. And yet a good percentage survived. It's kind of miraculous. But it was gruesome. Like a scene out of hell. The amputated limbs were thrown onto piles. What else could they do with them? Such carnage. Antietam. Gettysburg.
But then you go to these places today and it's so tranquil. It has the kind of beauty that can only be described as peaceful. And that's true of almost every battlefield I've ever visited. Anywhere in the world.

(ANTON *stops, charged by the mystery of it. He looks at* LIBBY *who has been observing him.*)

LIBBY: You're glowing, Anton.

ANTON: Glowing?

LIBBY: You're all lit up.

ANTON: Lit up?

LIBBY: It's like it's holy for you.

ANTON: It's my profession, Libby. I'm a historian. And I'm communicating, okay? I'm alive, is that all right? I'm telling you about something that means something to me. Something I've devoted many hours of my life to examining. There are things that I have studied and they have meaning. They mean something to me. And no one can take that away from me. I won't let you. I won't let anybody.

LIBBY: I'm not *taking* anything. You gave me the lesson, Anton. On the dead and dying. And suddenly you spring to life. That's all. That's all I'm saying.

ANTON: What's that supposed to mean?

LIBBY: You tell me. But think about it first.

ANTON: No. Libby. I won't think about it first. I'm tired of thinking first. And first and foremost of you. Of thinking about you above all else.

LIBBY: No one told you to.
And go fuck yourself with your "hallowed battlegrounds"!

ANTON: I never used those words!

LIBBY: But it's what you think.

ANTON: Whoa. Wait a minute. You can't do that. You cannot imply something like that of me. You have no right. You don't know me. You don't know what I am thinking. How I feel about things. How I—

LIBBY: Admit it, Anton. War's your religion.

ANTON: Don't do this

LIBBY: War gives you "meaning", like you say. Though you never fought in one yourself. Or did you?
(*Observing him, quickly*)
No. I didn't think so.

ANTON: Oh, no. No. Uh, huh. I don't understand. I don't understand what you want from me. You asked me to tell you about the Civil War. So I do. What am I not getting? I swear I don't know what you're asking for. Or what game you're playing. Is everything I say a weapon to be used against me?

LIBBY: I don't even exist for you. Not really. You're some kind of foot soldier in your mind. Fighting some damn holy battle. You're a warrior on a crusade. I get it

now. You're not just a healer, no. You're not just some
fucking miracle-worker. And by the way, I've got news
for you there.
You never picked your car off me alone. There were
others on the scene. They lifted it with you. Some of
them visit me, too. You all did it together. I'm not
saying you're a liar. You just didn't see the others.

ANTON: *(Accepting this)* No.

LIBBY: There are no miracles, Anton.

(ANTON turns away. But LIBBY's not finished with him.)

LIBBY: So, how come battlefields are peaceful?

(A pause)

ANTON: I don't have an answer for that, Libby.
(Turning on her) And don't you dare try and tell me.
I'm sick of your answers. I'm sick of your questions.
I'm sick of your revenge. Of your reproaches. Look at
you. You don't even have a fucking memory. And you
think you can tell me? You're just a playground bully.
I've met you more than once in my life, believe me. But
I pity you, I do. I pity you terribly. That's really all I
feel. And it's exhausting. Pity and guilt. It's wiping me
out. It's nauseating. You think that's attractive? You
think that's appealing? Your pain. Your fury. You've
got no grace, Libby. Maybe it's true, like you said.
There are no accidents. Maybe I was sent to run you
down. Before you crushed the next poor bastard.

(LIBBY takes this in. She struggles to get up, but can't.)

ANTON: You're damaged goods. Look at you. You're a
fucking wreck. You're pitiful. I hate you, Libby. I can't
stand the sight of you.

(LIBBY is struggling to get up.)

ANTON: What are you doing????

LIBBY: I'm going to kill you.

(She tries to get up. She can't. It's tortuous.)
I'm going to rip you apart.

ANTON: Are you? Are you, Libby? Oh, yeah? Really?
Look at you. Libby. Look at you. You're a fucking
cripple. You can't touch me.

*(Somehow LIBBY hurls herself off the bed with a blood-
curdling roar onto ANTON. She screams with the pain and
terror of it. He catches her, shocked. He holds her up by her
arms. Upright for the first time since her accident, she passes
out for a split second, her head falling back, then comes to.
She begins to whimper. This goes on for some time.)*

ANTON: Libby.

*(There is silence. LIBBY is held upright by ANTON. It takes
all his strength and concentration.)*

LIBBY: *(Defeated)* I'm gonna kill you.

ANTON: Right.

LIBBY: *(Quietly)* I'm gonna rip you apart

(A pause. ANTON makes a decision.)

ANTON: *(Gently)* Lift your left hand.

(LIBBY does, somehow, and then puts it down.)

ANTON: Lift your right hand.

(LIBBY does, then lets it drop.)

ANTON: Lift your right foot.

(LIBBY can, with huge effort)

ANTON: Left foot.

(LIBBY does.)

ANTON: Right foot.
Left.
Right.
Left.

Right. Left!

Stop, Libby!

(LIBBY *doesn't.*)

ANTON: That's enough.

(LIBBY *doesn't stop. She keeps on marching in place.* ANTON *gives in, marches with her, holding her up by her arms. The marching together—body-to-body—in this intense, martial rhythm continues for some time.*)

(*End of scene*)

Scene

(LIBBY *sits in a wheelchair.* ANTON *sits in a chair across from her.*)

LIBBY: Whatcha gonna do, Anton?

ANTON: Do when, Libby?

LIBBY: When I recover.

ANTON: You *have* recovered. Look at you! You're a miracle, whatever you say. Everybody says so.

LIBBY: When I can walk again, I mean. On my own.

ANTON: We'll take a long walk! I'm counting the days.

LIBBY: When I can go home.

ANTON: We'll throw such a party! We'll dance until dawn.

LIBBY: I'll run so far away from here.
(*She looks at him.*)
From you.

ANTON: You don't think I know that? I know you will. I'll never see you again, I bet.

LIBBY: And that's okay with you?

(ANTON *nods.*)

ANTON: At first, we'll meet regularly—at longer and longer intervals, and then sporadically. And then, when you're completely healed, you won't need me. You won't even remember my name.
And I won't need you, either.

LIBBY: Is healing that cruel?

ANTON: It's necessary.

LIBBY: That cold?
I feel you slipping away. People don't change.

ANTON: How so? I'm by your side.
And I'll stay there. Wherever you are. In a hard chair by your bed. You won't be able to get rid of me.
Just kidding, Libby.
(A pause)
In the summer, you're going wild apple-picking in Kazakhstan. And I won't worry about you, at all.
Nothing bad can happen to you there. You know why?

LIBBY: No.

ANTON: Because I'll be on the other side of the world!

(ANTON *and* LIBBY *enjoy this. A pause)*

ANTON: Apropos of that. I'm driving again.

LIBBY: Anton!

ANTON: I got into the car. And I began to shake. I couldn't grip the wheel for shaking, but I was shaking all over. My hands were pouring sweat. Everything was streaming down.
(He can't go on, then he can.)
I couldn't get the key in. I couldn't get it in. But I didn't give up.

LIBBY: Take me for a drive!

(ANTON *looks at* LIBBY.)

ANTON: I drove around the high school parking lot. Like a teenager. Learning it all for the very first time. I even felt a little rush. A little thrill of freedom.

LIBBY: Let's go for a ride. Get a milkshake! Let's take a road trip!

ANTON: One day, Libby.

LIBBY: Let's go today. I want to see Sante Fe! Let's drive off. Get in the car and head off!

ANTON: (*A pause, he makes a decision. He pulls his chair over next to her and sits.*) Buckled up?

LIBBY: Yup.

ANTON: We're heading out. The Sante Fe Trail.

LIBBY: We're on the highway, heading up into the Sangre de Cristo Mountains.

ANTON: We're on the range now, circling. Higher and higher.

LIBBY: Faster, Anton, go faster!

ANTON: I can't, Libby! I'll lose control!

LIBBY: Lose it, Anton! Pump the gas, man! Shit, let me drive. You big fat baby. Faster, faster.

ANTON: I don't like heights, Libby. I don't like speed. Let me slow down, please. Speed limit 15, Libby. Speed limit 10.

LIBBY: You're scared. I'm turning the wheel, Anton. Off we go. We're in the sky now. Falling, falling, falling. Then flying, flying. We're flying. I look at you and you look at me. And it's okay. Isn't it, Anton?

ANTON: It's okay.

(*A long pause.* ANTON *breaks down, from exhaustion, despair, joy, love. He weeps.*)

(End of scene)

Scene

(LIBBY sits on a regular chair looking out the window. A small bag by her side. ANTON stands behind her.)

ANTON: I'm disturbing you.

(LIBBY turns to face ANTON.)

LIBBY: No, Anton. It's okay.
Big news today.
I'm leaving this place. I got the go ahead. I got the green light.

ANTON: Oh. Oh. That's fantastic news, Libby.

LIBBY: They found me. Those people who love me. Like you said.
(There is a pause, she begins. It spills out.)
Guess what, Anton? I left my lover. I left my job. —I was working in T V, Anton. Can you imagine? I'd been sucked in. I'd completely forgotten— I walked out. Just took off. Cut loose. Left everything. Left it all behind. Don't call me, I told them. I'll call you. When I'm ready to. I need some time. Make a new beginning, I thought. Start over. Find out who you really are. Somewhere else. Somewhere far. That's how I landed here. There's an irony in there, don't you think?

ANTON: Something good will come of this. Something new, with time.

LIBBY: Something new, indeed.
They started me on Trauma therapy.
Because my memory is coming back.
The memory of that day is coming back.

(ANTON turns away.)

LIBBY: It wasn't a bad day, Anton. The sun was shining.
I was in a good mood.
I was on the top of the world that day.
In fact, I had never felt better.
I had to buy some new shoes. I had to get my hair cut.
But first. I had to run to the bank.

ANTON: Please, Libby.

LIBBY: It wasn't a bad day. But how can you start a day
and end it here. It was a *questionable* day.

(A pause. ANTON braces himself.)

LIBBY: I was texting my lover. It's all come back, Anton,
I can remember. To say it had all been a big mistake. To
say I was coming home.

(ANTON sits down on the bed. There is silence.)

LIBBY: That's what I was doing. When this thing
happened.

(ANTON drops his head.)

LIBBY: Anton!

(ANTON looks up.)

LIBBY: I want to see you smile.

(ANTON shrugs.)

LIBBY: The accident ward is full of folk with bad
luck. It's often a vacation that trips you up. You'd be
surprised. The streets are unfamiliar. You're more
vulnerable.
And of course, it's your own fault or the fault of some
other asshole, sorry, Anton. So no one really feels that
sorry for you. Not like in the other wards.

*(This makes ANTON smile. They smile at each other for
some time, watching each other smile. With concentration,
but simply, LIBBY gets up. She stands there without any
support. There is something terrifying and powerful about*

it. He looks at her like he is witnessing a specter. He makes no move to help her. He watches her. With care, she puts her bag on her shoulder. And then haltingly, like a baby who has just learned to take its first steps, she walks toward him. She stands over him.)

ANTON: Libby.

LIBBY: After a battle, the field heals.
That's why it's peaceful. Anton.

(ANTON takes this in. He nods, but says nothing. LIBBY is leaving.)

ANTON: Libby!

(LIBBY stops.)

ANTON: Watch where you're going next time, okay?

(LIBBY nods. They take each other in. ANTON turns away.)

(LIBBY leaves.)

(Left alone, ANTON lies back on the bed. And in an action which feels neither sudden nor unnatural, though he is fully dressed, he covers himself with the sheet, pulling himself into a fetal position. He stays like this for some time. But then he gets up. And slowly looking around the room, he leaves. The room stands empty. A rendering of The Battle Hymn of the Republic *reminiscent of the Civil War is heard.)*

(End of Scene)

END OF PLAY